SNAKES AND REPTILES

MINDFULNESS MEDITATION
ADULT
COLORING BOOK

ASSEMBLED BY
MADDIE MAYFAIR

ISBN-13: 978-1542489959

ISBN-10: 1542489954

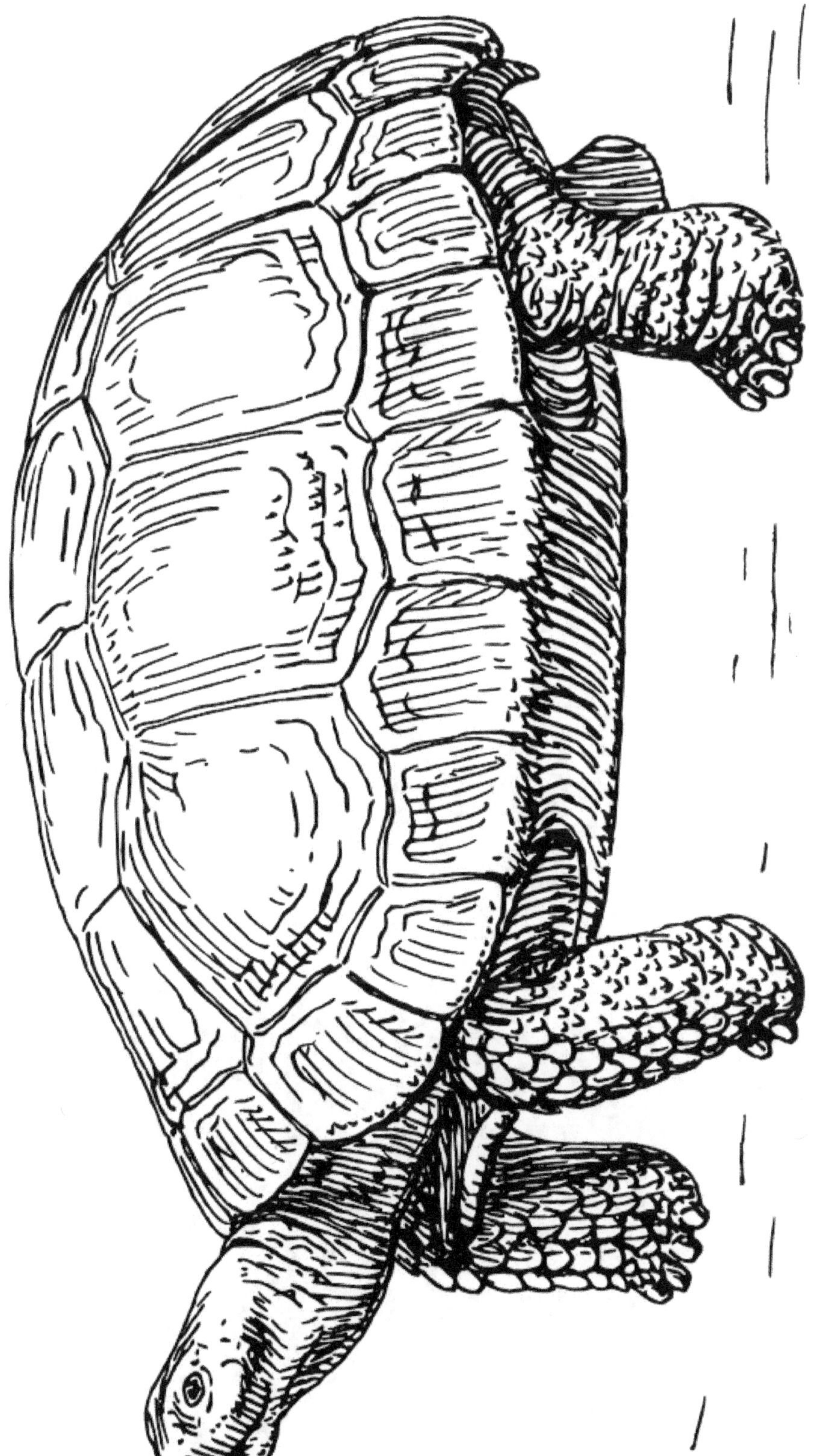

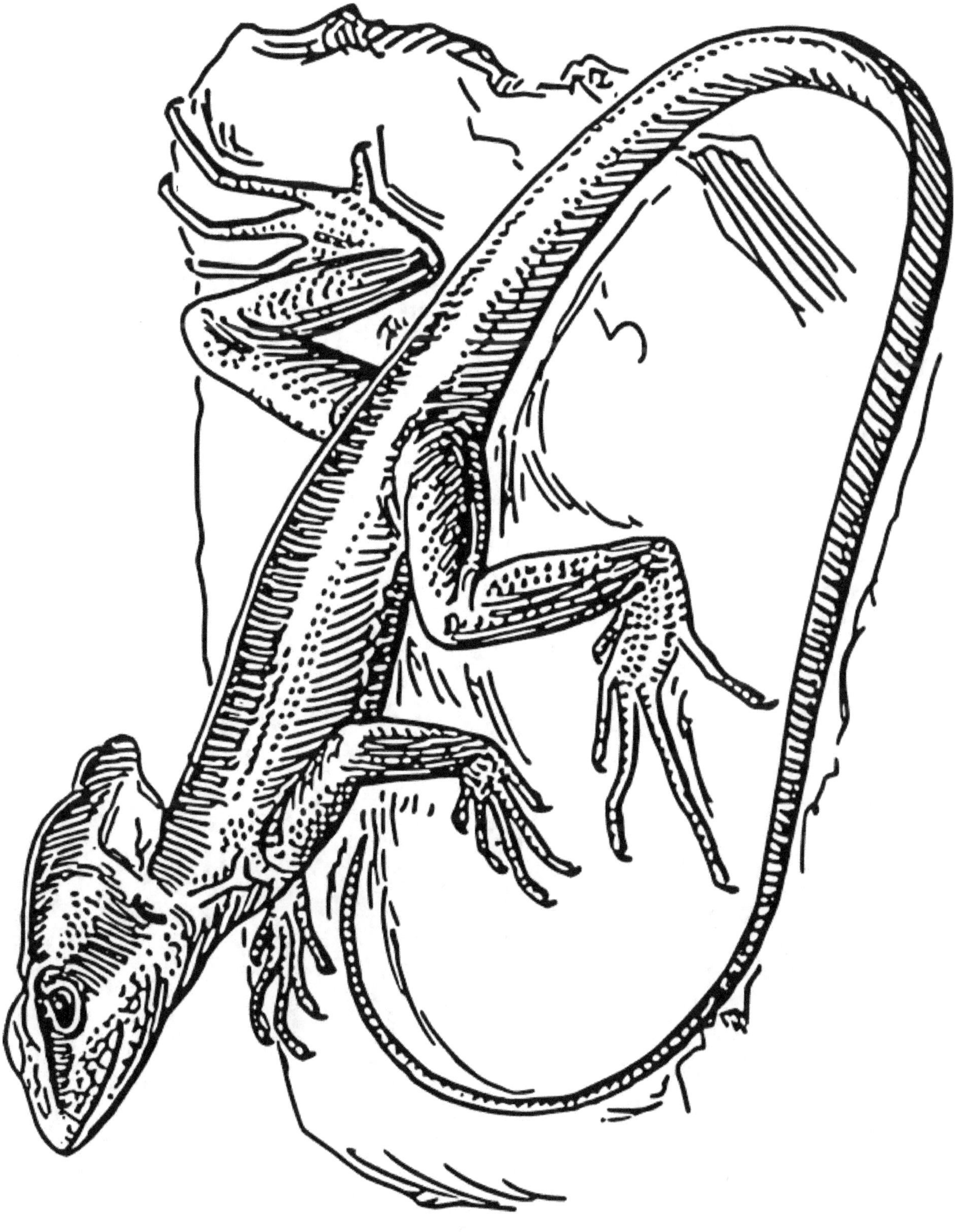

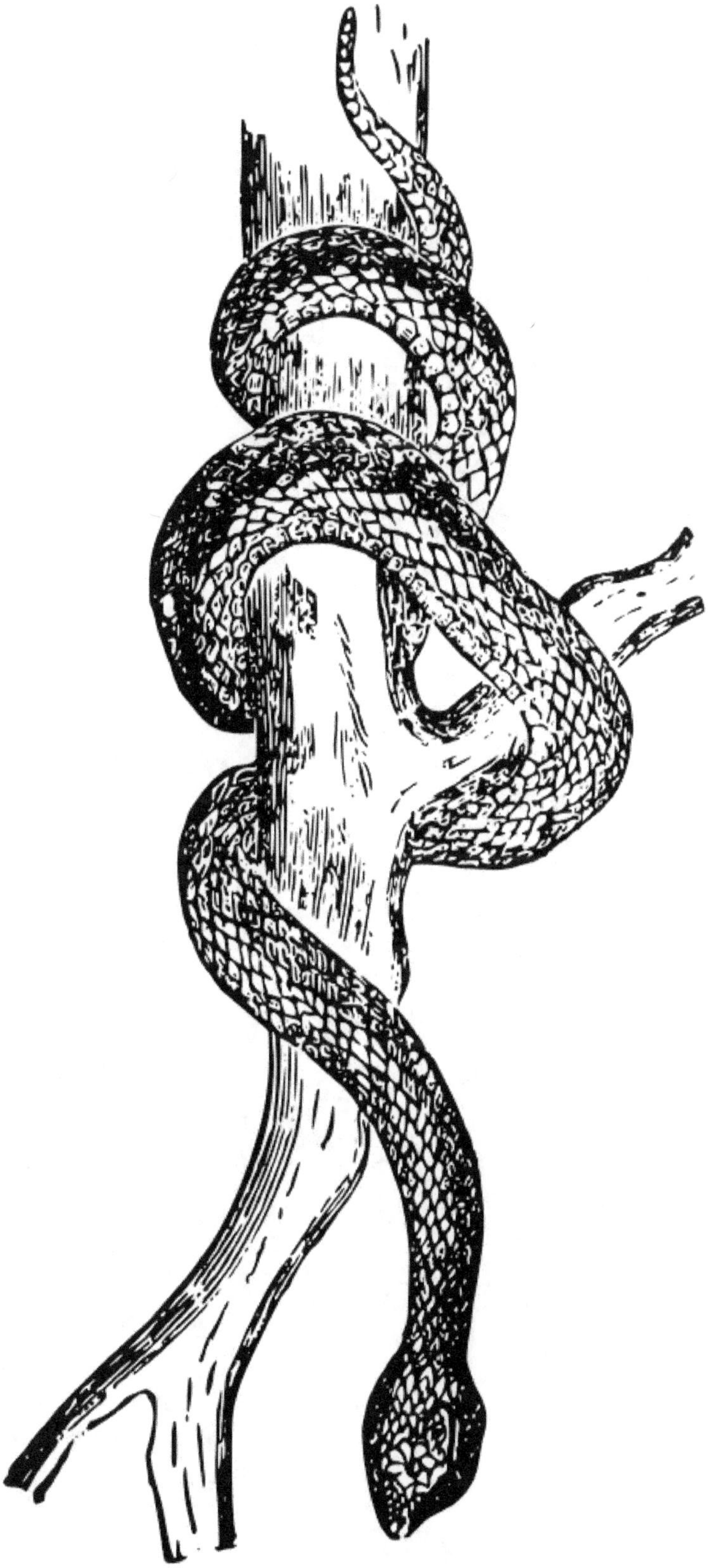

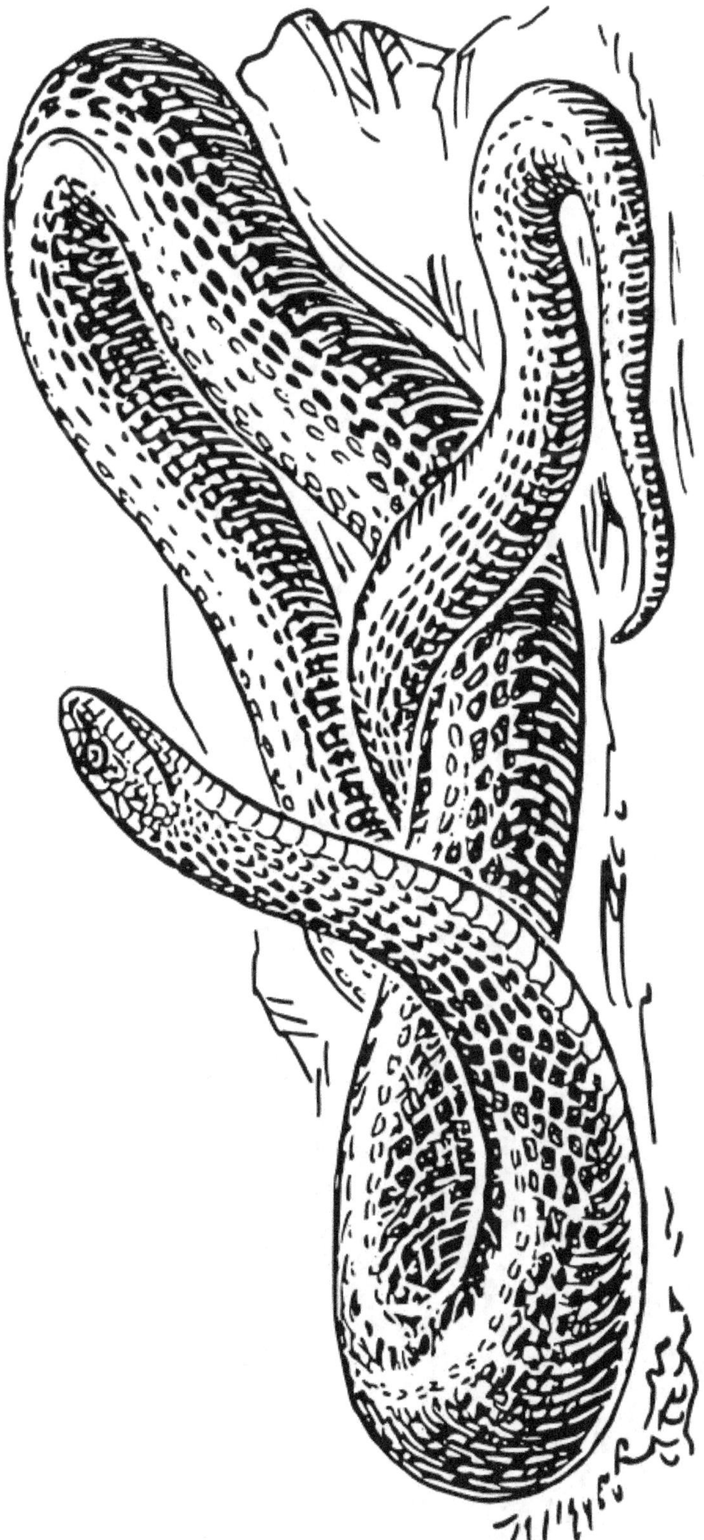

Enjoy even more *Colouring Books for Grown-Ups,* including:

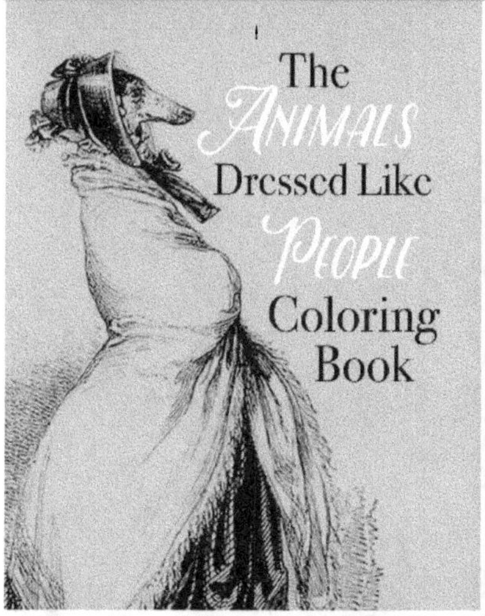

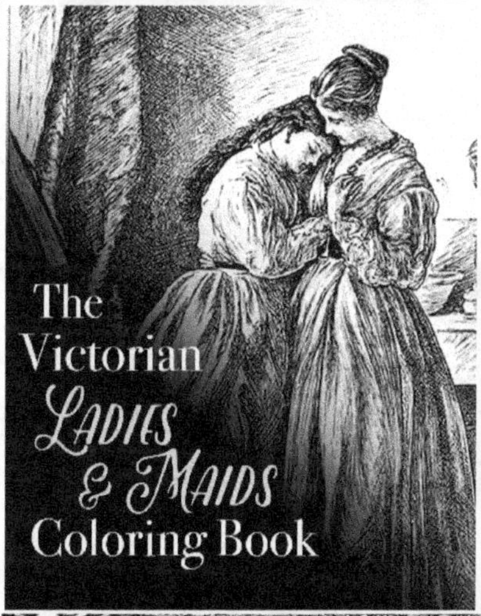

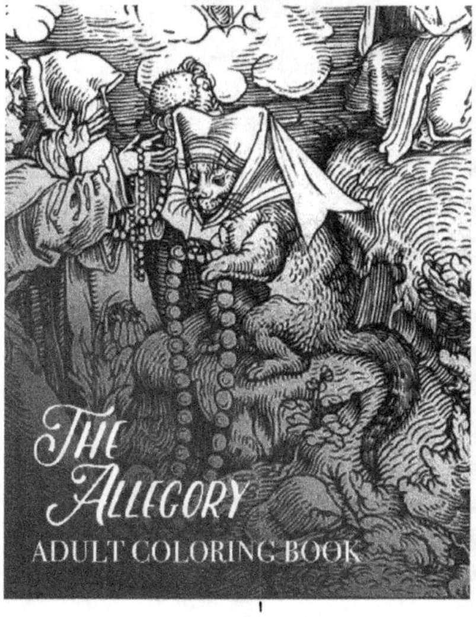

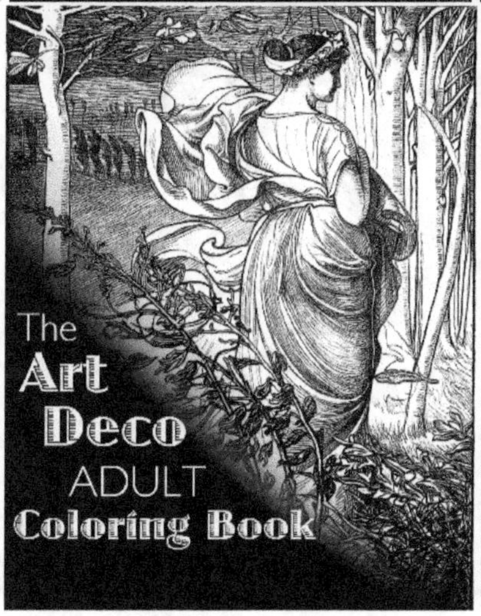

www.ingramcontent.com/pod-product-compliance
Lightning Source LLC
Chambersburg PA
CBHW081538280526
45788CB00010B/3280
9781542489959